CHILLING
WITH
GHOSTS

CHILLING WITH
GHOSTS

By Insha Fitzpatrick

Illustrations by Lilla Bölecz

A TOTALLY FACTUAL

· FIELD GUIDE TO THE ·
SUPERNATURAL

QUIRK BOOKS

PHILADELPHIA

Library of Congress Cataloging-in-Publication Data
Names: Fitzpatrick, Insha, author. | Bölecz, Lilla, illustrator.
Title: Chilling with ghosts : a totally factual field guide to the supernatural / by Insha Fitzpatrick ; illustrations by Lilla Bölecz.
Description: Philadelphia : Quirk Books, [2023] | Includes bibliographical references. | Audience: Ages 8-12 | Audience: Grades 4-6 | Summary: "An illustrated nonfiction guide to ghosts in history, legend, and pop culture"— Provided by publisher.
Identifiers: LCCN 2022060117 (print) | LCCN 2022060118 (ebook) | ISBN 9781683693451 (paperback) | ISBN 9781683693468 (ebook)
Subjects: LCSH: Ghosts—Juvenile literature.
Classification: LCC BF1461 .F588 2023 (print) | LCC BF1461 (ebook) | DDC 133.1— dc23/eng/20230214
LC record available at https://lccn.loc.gov/2022060117
LC ebook record available at https://lccn.loc.gov/2022060118

ISBN: 978-1-68369-345-1

Printed in China

Typeset in Black Magic, Freight, Fright Night, and Wolfsbane

Designed by Andie Reid
Illustrations by Lilla Bölecz
Production management by John J. McGurk

Quirk Books
215 Church Street
Philadelphia, PA 19106
quirkbooks.com

10 9 8 7 6 5 4 3 2 1

*To the spookiest editor
and a fellow nerd, Jessica*

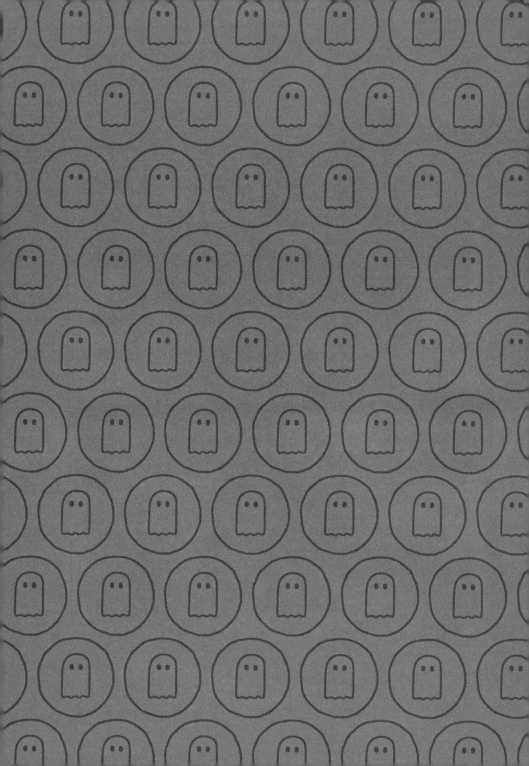

CONTENTS

DO YOU BELIEVE IN GHOSTS?

BOO! Scared you, didn't I? No? You're a tough one, I can tell. (But for the record, it's totally okay and perfectly normal to be scared sometimes. That's just life.) Since you're here, pull up a log and join me by the campfire. Okay, so there's no campfire. Just imagine one—flickering flames, a starry sky, and the smell of toasted marshmallows. Get ready for some thrills and chills—we're here to talk all things ghosts!

WHO ARE YOU, AGAIN?

Nice to meet you, [*insert super cool name here*]. I'm your personal guide to the awesome, scary, and weird world of the supernatural. In this book, we'll be covering everything you need to know about ghosts. We'll explore haunting history, spooky science, and terrifying tales. Along the way, we'll whip up ghostly snacks, craft our own ghost stories, and so much more.

Dig Out the Dictionary!

According to our friend Merriam-Webster, a ghost is "a disembodied soul; especially the soul of a dead person believed to be an inhabitant of the unseen world or to appear to the living in bodily likeness." When we talk about ghosts in this guide, we'll be discussing the spirit of a deceased person that haunts a place, person, or object.

HOLD YOUR PHANTOMS! ARE GHOSTS REAL?!

You might be thinking, "Hang on, are ghosts even real? Why is this book in the nonfiction section? And what's for lunch again?" Before we step onto the spectral plane, let's set things straight.

Throughout this guide, we'll be covering facts and legends about ghosts—tales of haunted locales, ghosts in literature and media, real-life history and science, and much more. But are ghosts real? Well, here's the thing: Beliefs regarding ghosts and death are incredibly personal and rooted in culture, religion, and values. The question isn't if ghosts are real. The question is do *you* believe in them?

You, dear reader, might be a believer. Maybe you've even had a ghost encounter! Or you might be a skeptic, a.k.a. someone who doubts the existence of ghosts but isn't totally sure. Or you might be firmly in the camp of "there's absolutely no way ghosts exist." Whatever you think, I welcome you on this supernatural quest for knowledge.

According to Science

In a 2021 YouGov survey of one thousand people, 41 percent of the survey group said that they believed in the existence of ghosts . . . and 20 percent said that they had personally encountered a ghost!

Ghosts represent a lot to many people. Their stories can connect us to the past, tell us about our fears, and help us understand the unknown. So let's pull out our flashlights and shine a light on the unseen world of ghosts. We'll answer questions like: What do ghosts symbolize? What role do ghosts play in different cultures? Can bathrooms be haunted?

Ready to answer some questions? Turn the page . . . if you dare!

Chapter 1

GHOSTS 101

What is a ghost?
Something dead that
seems to be alive.
Something dead that
doesn't know it's dead.

—Richard Siken

Welcome to Ghosts 101! On the syllabus we've got all the spectral basics: What makes a ghost a ghost? How do you identify a ghost? What are the different types of ghosts? Where do ghosts like to hang out? Pick up that lantern over there and come with me as we step into the night.

HOW TO IDENTIFY A GHOST

When you imagine a ghost, what do you think of? Do you picture someone draped in white bedsheets with two cut-outs for eyes, trick-or-treating on the street? Or do you envision a ghastly apparition dripping with green ectoplasm (a.k.a. a paranormal substance said to allow spirits to materialize)? Maybe you're thinking of a translucent version of a regular person who looks just like you and me.

According to Lisa Morton, author of the book *Ghosts: A Haunted History*, "the shape the undead spirit takes varies according to the particular society's collective imagination." What you think a ghost looks like depends on your context! But in general, Western ghost stories have a few key traits in common. Let's go over these key ghostly characteristics.

Noncorporeal

I'm corporeal. You're corporeal—or at least I hope you are! Being corporeal means that you have a physical body. Ghosts are spirits, and they don't have a physical body. That's why in ghost stories, they are often depicted as semitransparent and able to float through walls. For the most part, ghosts can't interact with the physical world. You're probably not going to catch one scarfing down a bag of chips or playing the piano . . . but of course, there are exceptions. (More on that later!)

HOW TO IDENTIFY A GHOST

Ye Olde History

What is a soul? You can define a soul in a variety of ways, and countless philosophers have grappled with this question. Philosophers of the past such as Aristotle, Immanuel Kant, René Descartes, and Plato all have different theories on what a soul is and if souls are even real. A simple definition of the soul is the spiritual essence of a person (or animal!) that is a core part of them that sticks around after their physical body dies. Here's one more philosopher for you: Pythagoras. Born in 570 BCE, Pythagoras was a Greek philosopher who believed that when a person dies, their soul leaves their body and jumps into a whole new body. But he wasn't just famous for his theories on the soul. The Pythagorean theorem ($a^2 + b^2 = c^2$) is named after him!

Haunting Appearance

Ghosts are generally spooky looking. They might appear as they did when they passed away. Or they might look like whatever appearance captures their essence. They might not even look like a human—they might resemble a see-through zombie or a ball of light!

Ability to Float or Fly

Given that ghosts are noncorporeal, gravity doesn't exactly apply to them. In most tales, ghosts can walk through walls, float above the ground, and even fly.

Limited Interaction with the Physical World

Generally, ghosts can't interact with the physical world, but there are exceptions. Depending on the account, some ghosts can speak, move objects, or influence the environment in various ways, such as creating cold spots or giving off spooky vibes.

Terrifying Tales

Ever been to a haunted house? There's one in Atchison, Kansas, called the Sallie House. Built in the mid-1800s, the house was owned by a physician who operated on many patients. Sadly, some of these patients passed away inside the house, including a young girl named Sallie. Throughout the years, people visiting the Sallie House have claimed to see objects move, experience eerily cold spots, or feel an unseen presence scratch them.

SENSING GHOSTS

Have you heard the saying "seeing is believing"? With ghosts, it's the opposite—believing is seeing. If you believe in ghosts, you're more likely to see a spirit than someone who doesn't believe in them.

Some people have made a living out of interacting with the supernatural. *Mediums* are people who claim to be able to communicate between the living and the dead. They play a role in a variety of religions and cultural practices, including Shamanism and Spiritualism. Some people believe that mediums have real abilities, whereas others argue that it's all smoke and mirrors . . . A phenomenon called *confirmation bias* can influence whether or not someone believes everything a medium says.

According to Science

Don't you love being right? Confirmation bias is when you believe something to be true and you seek evidence or interpret information that proves you right. Basically, it's when you favor, or are *biased* toward, information that *confirms* your belief. But confirmation bias can lead to incorrect assumptions and dangerous conclusions. How can you beat confirmation bias? Make sure you get your news and facts from reliable, unbiased, and trusted sources . . . and keep your mind open!

But do you have to be a medium to see a ghost? According to most ghost lore, no! All types of people can have encounters of the spectral kind: relatives of the deceased, random bystanders, or people who are extra sensitive when it comes to the supernatural. It helps to have a deep connection to the ghost, or to strongly believe in the existence of ghosts.

Of course, seeing isn't everything. You might walk into a cold spot and feel a chill. You might get bopped with a floating object. You might hear a spooky wail. You might smell the smoke of candles suddenly snuffing out. There are many ways to sense a ghost.

According to Science

When you squeeze your eyes closed, do you ever see spots of light or color? Those spots are called phosphenes! Phosphenes can result when your retina, optic nerve, or visual cortex gets stimulated in some way. You might see phosphenes when you rub your eyes, cough really hard, blow your nose, or experience head trauma (please, please see a doctor if you experience head trauma). Talk about seeing stars!

TYPES OF GHOSTS

Now that we've covered the basics, let's talk about the various types of ghosts, depending on the ghost story.

Ghosts That Haunt

Some ghosts haunt the same places and do the same thing every day—kind of like a video on loop. This phenomenon is also known as *residual haunting*. You might've heard about these kinds of ghosts around a campfire or read a museum plaque about legends of a ghost haunting a battleground. These ghosts may have unfinished business or have died a wrongful, traumatic death. Signs that a residual ghost is hanging around include repetitive and mysterious noises such as footsteps, knocking, or strange voices.

Read All About It

The stone tape theory is the theory that stones and other objects in an environment can store and replay major emotional events—resulting in residual hauntings. The idea is that these hauntings play out like a cassette tape recording, a.k.a. a type of audio recording popular in the 1970s. This theory was popularized by the 1972 BBC drama *The Stone Tape*. The film takes place in an old haunted mansion, where scientists realize that the mansion's stones have recorded a terrible death.

Poltergeists

Poltergeist is German for "noisy spirit," and for a good reason: when poltergeists make their presence known, they do it with a bang! They're known for causing major disturbances—loud noises in the night, unexpected fires, and levitating furniture. They're even said to scratch, bite, or hit people! *Yikes*.

Ghost Lights

Ghost lights are described in ghost stories as little balls of light that appear seemingly from nowhere. Types of ghost lights include will-o'-the-wisp, or corpse lights, and onibi. Will-o'-the-wisp is said to appear at night in remote areas such as marshes or bogs. And according to Japanese folklore, onibi are blue ghost lights that come from corpses.

According to Science

Bioluminescence (light emitted by living organisms) and chemi-luminescence (light produced by chemical reactions) are two possible explanations for sightings of mysterious ghost lights. One example of bioluminescence is the *Noctiluca scintillans*, also called sea sparkle or sea ghost, which is a type of sea-dwelling plankton. (Specifically, it's a species of dinoflagellate, a single-celled marine microorganism.) They light up when they're disturbed by any kind of movement, like a crashing wave or someone walking in the water. The result is a bright blue light that can sometimes be seen at night.

These are just a few of the forms ghosts have taken in spooky stories and haunting legends. But there are more, such as:

- **Mists:** Mist is the result of water vapor meeting cold air and transforming from a gas into water droplets. Some people have claimed to glimpse ghostly faces in mist.
- **Orbs of light:** Unexplained spots of light in photos or seen in real life have been attributed to ghosts taking this form.
- **Possessed objects:** In some ghost stories, ghosts are said to possess objects . . . or even people (creepy!).
- **Shadow figures:** Ghosts in this form appear as (surprise, surprise) shadowy figures. You might see one out of the corner of your eye or captured in a photograph. (Seeing shadow figures

has been attributed to a variety of conditions, such as hallucinations occurring during sleep paralysis.)

- **Funnel ghosts:** Brrrr! Anyone feel a chill? Funnel ghosts take the form of a swirling light or funnel and often leave a chilly spot in their wake.
- **Ghost pets:** If people can be ghosts, why not pets? Plenty of ghost stories feature animal ghosts, including pets. Scary or cute? You decide.

FAVORITE HAUNTS AND HANGOUTS

As we've established, ghosts usually haunt a particular place. You don't often hear of ghosts hopping on planes and flying to Paris for vacation! But why do they stick to one spot? Common explanations include:

- The ghost haunts its final resting place.
- The ghost tragically died in the place that it haunts.
- The ghost lingers in an area where it has unfinished business to attend to.
- The site the ghost is haunting has deep meaning for them, and they don't want to leave.

Any place can be haunted—yes, even the bathroom. Of course, some places are linked to far more ghost sightings and stories than others. Following are the top destinations for ghosts.

Cemeteries

Since ghosts are known for haunting their final resting place, cemeteries and graveyards are where many tales of ghost sightings are set. (What's the difference between a cemetery and a graveyard? A cemetery is a burial ground, whereas a graveyard is a burial place near or inside a churchyard.) The St. Louis Cemetery No.1, the oldest cemetery in New Orleans, is notorious for being haunted. A number of notable figures are buried there, including Marie Laveau, a famous

Voodoo practitioner from the 1800s. Even the actor Nicolas Cage wants to be buried there. He's already bought himself a pyramid mausoleum!

Homes

Home is where the heart is—and where the ghost haunts! Ghosts may linger in their homes because they're attached to them, or because they have unfinished business there, or because they died tragically there. Homes can include all types of places, even giant mansions and old castles. Some famously haunted homes include Burg Wolfsegg, a castle in Germany, and Raynham Hall, a mansion in England.

Battlefields

In some ghost stories, hauntings are attributed to trauma and tragic deaths. Battlefields are places of conflict, injustice, and tragedy—and they appear in many legends of the spectral kind. A few sites of battle that are said to be haunted include:

- **The Alamo Mission in San Antonio, Texas:** the site of the Battle of the Alamo, which lasted thirteen days in 1836 during the Texas Revolution
- **Zone Rouge in northeastern France:** a series of World War I battlefields that after the war was designated unsafe for humans to inhabit
- **The Colosseum in Rome, Italy:** the amphitheater, commissioned in 70 to 72 CE, that hosted gladiator matches, executions, plays, and reenactments of battles for entertainment for more than 50,000 people

Hotels

Hotels generally aren't considered homes (unless you're a character in the TV show *The Suite Life of Zack and Cody*), but can they be haunted? Dear reader, they sure can! Hotels—where many people come and go—are a hot spot for ghostly sightings and urban legends.

Ye Olde History

Have you heard of the Battle of Gettysburg? This bloody conflict took place during the American Civil War in Gettysburg, Pennsylvania, from July 1 to July 3, 1863. During the battle, the Union army, commanded by General George G. Meade, defeated the Confederate army, led by Robert E. Lee. The third day was the bloodiest, but it was an early sign of victory for the Union army, who finally triumphed in 1865. The Gettysburg battlefield is said to be haunted; visitors have reported seeing the ghosts of soldiers and hearing the sounds of fighting.

IT'S ALL IN YOUR HEAD ... OR IS IT?

Whenever you encounter something strange, mysterious, or inexplicable, that's a great opportunity to uncover the "why" behind it. Why are ghosts said to haunt a specific place? What kind of people appear in ghost stories? Why are tragedy and conflict linked with hauntings? What does believing in ghosts and ghost stories say about us as human beings? And why do some people—maybe that includes you!—believe in ghosts?

The answers are rarely straightforward. Take the last question, for example: why do some people believe in ghosts? Could individual beliefs be tied to religious and cultural practices that honor one's ancestors? Or could belief in ghosts come from a deep-rooted desire to explain the unexplainable? What about compelling personal experiences? Or maybe it's all just a weird dream or sleep paralysis or fireflies that look like ghost lights. Who knows?

Whew! That's a lot to think about. Take a deep breath, grab a snack, and do a few stretches. We're in this for the long haul, and we're not done yet! You've learned all the ghost basics, so it's time to level up. After your break, head to Chapter 2, where we'll be communicating with and busting ghosts. Hypothetically speaking, of course.

Ye Olde History

If you've ever wanted to visit a place with a haunted history, you can sign up to take a ghost tour. Ghost tours are curated events that teach you about a haunted place. Research whether there's a ghost tour in your city—there likely is! And remember to be respectful when you visit haunted sites, particularly because they are often places where tragedy has occurred.

Top 10 Signs You're Being Haunted

Are you being haunted? Hopefully not! But just to be sure, read up on the top ten signs that you're being haunted.

1. You feel like you're being watched, but no one else is in the room with you. (I know, spooky!)

2. You enter a room, and the temperature changes suddenly without explanation.

3. There's a cold spot in a specific place in your home . . . and it's not the AC malfunctioning.

4. Your pet—cat, dog, iguana, etc.—stares at seemingly nothing, refuses to enter a room, or bark/meows/makes whatever noise iguanas make at an unseen presence. (Mine does, and it creeps me out!)

5. Objects in your home keep appearing in places you didn't leave them, and it's not just your sibling making a mess.

6. You hear unexplained sounds in your home—like mysterious whispering, water running, or the floorboards creaking—when no one is awake.

7. Doors and windows open and close themselves without anyone touching them. Automatic doors don't count!

8 You smell new and lingering odors that seem to come from nowhere. (If that smell is moldy and gross, you might just need to clean out your fridge.)

9 Your electronics (TV, video game console, your mom's vintage vinyl player, etc.) turn on and off by themselves.

10 A ghost keeps hanging around you and won't leave you alone.

If you checked off every single one of those signs, you might just be haunted. Or it could a broken heater, noisy neighbors, a heavy door, and your friend dressed up as a ghost for Halloween. Who can say? Not me. I don't know your life! But hypothetically, if you're being haunted, what can you do about it? Keep reading to find out!

Chapter 2

HOW TO BUST A GHOST

Spengler, are you
serious about actually
catching a ghost?

—Peter Venkman,
Ghostbusters (1984)

So, let's say one day you wake up feeling haunted. No, not haunted by that horror movie you watched last night or by a creeping sense of existential dread, but haunted by a real-deal ghost. What do you do? You could ignore the ghost, sure, but trust me when I say that ignoring your problems doesn't ever work out. You have to face your ghosts (and problems) head-on. Prepare yourself, future supernaturalist, as we explore the world of the living and the dead!

HOW DO GHOSTS BECOME GHOSTS?

As we established in Chapter 1, a ghost is a "disembodied soul" or "the soul of a dead person." But how do ghosts end up as ghosts in the first place? The key to this question lies in common beliefs about death, the afterlife, your soul, and so much more.

Now, what you believe (or don't believe) about these things may be totally different from what someone else believes. It all depends on your cultural background, age, personal experiences, and countless other factors. There are so many different belief systems and ways of

understanding the world out there! I know, it's pretty neat. We'll get into some of these different traditions and beliefs later in this guide, but for now we're going to dive into common Western ghost lore.

Life After Death

What happens after death? As you've likely learned in science class (or from *Hanging with Vampires*, the first book in the Totally Factual Field Guide to the Supernatural series), the body starts to decompose. Yeah, it might be gross, but that's the cycle of life! Since ancient times, philosophers (and everyday people like you and me) have asked another question: what happens to your *soul*—if we have one at all—after death?

The answer varies. In some religions the belief is that the soul ends up in heaven or hell, while according to others the soul is reincarnated and comes back in another body and life. Still others believe that the soul goes to live in a type of underworld.

According to Science

A 2021 study by the Pew Research Center revealed that 7 percent of Americans believe in some kind of afterlife, and 17 percent don't.

The idea of the soul is where the concept of ghosts comes from. In Western culture, ghosts are generally seen as the souls of the dead who are meant to move on to the afterlife—but who made a pit stop along the way instead. Why would a ghost linger in the world of the living? Here are a few reasons.

1 **They have unfinished business.** According to various ghostly tales, unfinished business is one major reason why ghosts stay behind. The spirit might feel like they still need to do certain things or feel dissatisfied in some way. Maybe a ghost stays behind to watch over his husband or pass along an important message, like "I love you" or "don't forget to take out the trash." Ghosts with unfinished business will stick around until that task is done—whether it's resolving a disagreement or solving a murder.

To Do
- WALK THE DOG
- SCRUB THE TOILET
- SEE BEYONCÉ IN CONCERT
- BUY MORE AVOCADOS
- TRAVEL TO JAPAN
- WIN THE LOTTERY

2 **They're in denial about being dead.** Ghosts who keep hanging around may be in denial that they're dead. What might cause this? A sudden death or a death with mysterious causes.

3 **They died in a traumatic way.** In many ghost tales, you'll find that the ghost has a tragic origin story. The ghost may have died as a result of violence or in another terrible or shocking way. Their trauma and shock may make the ghost unable to move on. They might carry lingering fear, anger, or grief that prevents them from resting.

Okay, that was pretty heavy. You doing all right there? No? Take a break. Yes? Let's keep moving!

Now it's time to learn how to bust some hypothetical ghosts! Or chat with them in a respectful manner. Not everything can be resolved with busting, after all. And now that we understand how ghosts become ghosts, we know how to help them.

SPECTRAL TOOLS OF THE TRADE

In movies and books (and even in real life), people have dealt with ghosts in a whole bunch of different ways. The first step to dealing with ghosts is sensing them, since they're usually, y'know, kind of hard to see. Like the Little Mermaid, ghost experts have gadgets and gizmos aplenty. Here are just a few:

Dowsing rods: Used for divination (a.k.a. uncovering knowledge via magical, spiritual, or supernatural methods), dowsing rods are usually two small L-shaped rods that people throughout history have used to track down buried gems, metal, and jewels, along with groundwater and oil. Dowsing rods have also been used to locate ghosts or ask them questions. How do you use dowsing rods? Hold one rod in each hand, and then ask your question. If the rods cross, it's a yes

(and you've found some ghost energy!). If they don't, that's a no, so you'd then ask a different question! In the 2009 stop-motion movie *Coraline*, the main character uses a dowsing rod made of poison oak to find a well.

EMF meter: *EMF* stands for electromagnetic field, so an EMF meter is—you guessed it!—something that detects and measures electromagnetic fields. Electricians often carry these handy devices to check on appliances, power lines, and electrical wiring—but ghost hunters use them to determine if there is a spike or fall in electrical energy. If there is a spike, there's most likely a ghost in your midst. In the TV show *Supernatural* that aired during the 2000s, brothers Sam and Dean use EMF meters to detect ghosts, demons, and more.

Spirit box: This particular device skips through different radio channels when you turn it on. Spirits are thought to be able to break through the white noise to talk via the box, communicating with full sentences or a few words.

Proton pack: We can't talk about busting ghosts without talking about the one ghostly movie to rule them all. The proton pack made its debut in the 1984 *Ghostbusters* movie, and it's a portable particle accelerator equipped with a handheld wand, which is used to combine the negative energy that ghosts expel with positive ions from the machine. To capture their spectral foes, the Ghostbusters aimed the wand at ghosts, and the beam would pull them in!

"That's cool and all, but I don't live on the set of *Ghostbusters*," you might be saying. "This is real life!" Fair enough. You're unlikely to run into a green monster like Slimer on your way to school, but you never know when you might need to deal with the spooky and the unknown! And how do you deal with the unknown? Keep your mind open, learn as much as you can, and stay prepared! You've got the first two on lock. To help you with the third, we at Totally Factual Field Guide to the Supernatural HQ have exactly what you need ...

NOW INTRODUCING:

THE GHASTLY GHOSTLY TOOL KIT

Is your house haunted? Are you dealing with a ghost that won't leave you alone? Is your walk by the local graveyard just too spooky? Not to worry. The Ghastly Ghostly Tool Kit contains the gear you need to prepare for every supernatural and spectral eventuality!

---

1 **PHONE:** Camera, voice recorder, language translator, and flashlight—your phone (if you have one) has it all! Use your phone to take notes on your haunting observations, snap photos of your surroundings, shine a light on a darkened path, and play some tunes (maybe "Ghost Duet" by Louie Zong or "Somebody's Watching Me" by Rockwell). Who knows, maybe you'll catch a ghost in a selfie!

---

2 **INFRARED THERMOMETER:** Brrr! Did it just get cold in here? Quick, check the temperature! With a thermometer handy, you'll be able to measure cold spots or sudden temperature changes. Speaking of which, you'll definitely want to pack a...

---

3 **JACKET:** Whether you're strolling through a cemetery, crossing a chilly spot in a haunted house, or even getting blasted with ectoplasm, you'll need a cozy, protective jacket to keep you safe and warm. You won't regret it, rain or shine or gross ghost slime!

4 **SNACKS, SNACKS, AND MORE SNACKS:** Listen, investigating the supernatural isn't easy, and you can't do it on an empty stomach. Personally, I like to pack sour gummy worms wherever I go. It's smart to bring a snack (just like a good book)—Spam musubi, PB&J sandwiches, slices of lemon, whatever floats your boat—so you can chow down when the mood strikes.

5 **WATER BOTTLE:** Whether you're fleeing vengeful ghosts straight out of a Shakespearean play or just exploring a haunted house, you'll want to stay hydrated!

6 **NOTEBOOK OR SKETCHBOOK (AND PEN/PENCIL):** One great way to get to know your surroundings (and maybe some surrounding ghosts!) is to take notes. Pack a notebook so you can record what you see, smell, hear, and feel when you go somewhere ... or bring a sketchbook to draw your observations. And if you have a ghost run-in, you'll be ready to strike up a conversation and take notes.

7 **NEWSPAPER:** A current newspaper, specifically. If you encounter a confused ghost (or a time traveler) who doesn't know when or where they are, the date and current events in the newspaper will help them get situated in our day and age. And if you're ever bored, reading the newspaper can be interesting!

8 **THIS GUIDE:** In addition to the newspaper, this book will come in handy if you meet a confused ghost. Show this book to the ghost, and maybe they can figure out what their deal is. This guide is for humans, living and nonliving—all are welcome!

HOW TO TALK TO GHOSTS

While sucking up ghosts into a proton pack worked for the Ghost-busters, that's not always the best way to go about doing things. Remember when we talked about why ghosts end up as ghosts? Yep, you got it—unfinished business, a tragic death, or being in denial.

Looking at those common causes, does busting in to fight ghosts really sound like the solution? Yeah, I didn't think so! As with many regular, everyday problems, it's all about communication. Talking it out can solve a lot of issues, it turns out. Even with ghosts.

So if you hypothetically ran into a ghost, how would you talk to them? It's not as simple as strolling into a haunted house and shouting, "Hey ghosties, it's ya boy!" The key to talking to ghosts—or anyone, really—is to do so respectfully. After all, if we're operating on the belief that ghosts were once living beings, then we should be as respectful when talking to them as we are with anyone else—even if the ghost in question is an orb of light or a neon-purple ghost hippo with slime oozing out of its pores.

You may be saying, "Okay, cool, thanks for the etiquette lesson. But how do people talk to ghosts?" So glad you asked! Remember the mediums we talked about earlier? Some of these people claim that they can communicate with the dead or even look into the future, thanks to the aid of some handy communication tools. These include:

- **Ouija board:** Also known as a spirit board, the Ouija board was created in 1890 in Baltimore, Maryland. It features the numerals 0 through 9, the letters of the English alphabet, and the words YES and NO on the top and GOODBYE on the bottom. The board comes with a planchette (a small, heart-shaped piece of wood, resin, or glass) that users place their fingertips on, while spirits supposedly spell out their messages one character at a time.

- **Crystal ball:** This is a sphere made of glass or a crystal such as quartz used by certain people who claim they can see into the future, such as psychics, clairvoyants, and fortune tellers. Crystal balls are also popular props in stage magic routines.
- **Pendulum:** The kind of pendulum we're talking about here is a crystal that hangs from a long silver chain. Unlike the Ouija board, which allows spirits to spell out complex answers, the pendulum can only point to YES, NO, or MAYBE. The YES, NO, or MAYBE might be written on a sheet of paper, or the pendulum might be told that left means yes, right means no, and swinging in a circle means maybe.

These kinds of tools might get used during a séance, which you may be familiar with if you've watched horror movies. At a séance, a medium sits with other people with the intent to communicate with the dead. The word *séance* has its roots in the French word for "session"—so in English, a séance is a session with ghosts!

According to Science

In 1852, a scientist named William Benjamin Carpenter began investigating the use of dowsing rods, which were becoming increasingly popular thanks to the Spiritualism movement that took root in the US beginning in the 1840s. Carpenter noticed that mediums were experiencing what he called the ideomotor effect—*ideo*- meaning "idea" and -*motor* meaning "muscular action." The ideomotor effect is a psychological phenomenon in which your body moves unconsciously, or without your conscious choice. These unconscious movements might be influenced by what you believe or expect to happen. For example, someone using a Ouija board may think that a spirit is controlling the planchette, when in fact the person is the one moving the planchette unconsciously.

But for regular, nonmedium supernaturalists like you and me, it's best to avoid dabbling in things we don't fully understand. How we communicate with the supernatural is a little different . . .

WELCOME TO MY DEAD TALK

As fascinating as spectral beings are, it's usually best to leave them alone. Live and let live or, in the case of ghosts, live and let dead. Don't go looking for trouble! But let's say, hypothetically, that you're face-to-face with a ghost in your home, or there's a ghost haunting your science classroom, or you run into a ghost while taking a peaceful stroll through a cemetery . . . what do you do? How do you talk to ghosts? Let's break it down step by step!

1 Have your Ghastly Ghostly Tool Kit handy (see page 42). Pull on a jacket if you're chilly, have a snack—you'll need your strength!—and grab your phone, pen or pencil, and notebook.

2 Greet the ghost. After all, when you first meet someone, you don't launch straight into "pineapple on pizza, yea or nay?" You politely introduce yourself and get your conversation partner's name. When you talk to a ghost, it's the same deal—you have to acknowledge them first! "Hi, my name is [*insert awesome name here*]. It's nice to meet you. What's your name?" Easy, right? Then you will proceed in one of two ways:

- If the ghost stays calm and introduces themselves, then move on to Step 3!
- If the ghost doesn't seem like they want to talk to you, that's your sign to leave the ghost alone and get outta there. As much as you may want to, you can't force a conversation.

3 So the ghost is ready to talk. You might be scared, but hey, they might be, too. If you're not sure what to say, think about what your goal is for the conversation. Do you want to find out what's troubling the ghost? Or do you just want to get to know them? The key to communicating is to be willing to listen. Ask questions and listen to what the ghost has to say. Here are some questions you can ask your new phantom friend:

- What is your name?
- If you're comfortable, can you make yourself visible?
- Is there a different way you'd prefer to communicate other than talking?
- Do you live here? How long have you lived here?
- Do you have a message for me?
- Do you have a message for someone else?
- Is there something troubling you? How can I help you?
- If it's okay with you, could you tell me a little more about yourself and who you are?
- Is there anything you'd like to know about me?
- Do you want to be left alone? Do you want me to leave now?

4 Once you ask them a question, stay silent for a bit. Again, it's important to be a good listener. Use your gut and observational skills to look, listen, and sense things around you that may have shifted when you asked your question. It's all about actively listening and paying attention when talking to ghosts. (And if you notice that the vibes are off, that's your cue to make a graceful exit.)

GOODBYE, GHOST!

Let's say you talked to a ghost hanging out in your home and found out what they needed—maybe they wanted you to give their dog some belly scratches or pass a message along to their best friend. The ghost has since moved on, but you still feel unsettled. How do you make your home feel less, well, haunted? Good question! You'll want to refresh your space to make it feel like yours again.

There are plenty of things you can do! You could brew some delicious hot chocolate, cuddle up in your favorite sweater or blanket, or watch a movie that you find comforting. Why? The goal is to improve the atmosphere and vibe of your space. What better way to do that than to do something you enjoy? It's important to feel safe and cozy in your space.

Chill Vibes

Sometimes, even if we're not being haunted by literal ghosts, we experience feelings of unease, worry, or dread. Everyone goes through this, including me, your incredibly cool guide to the supernatural. You might feel anxious because of a scary or stressful situation—or for no reason at all. It happens! But what can you do when you're feeling a bit overwhelmed or anxious?

1. **Take deep breaths.** When you feel anxious, you might notice that your breathing gets faster and faster, or that your heart starts racing. Or maybe it's your mind that starts racing. Try taking some deep breaths. The easiest way to keep track of them is by counting. Inhale while slowly counting to four, and then exhale to a count of four again. Repeat this a few times until you feel like your breathing has calmed down.

2. **Go for a walk, drink some water, or listen to music.** Or try something else that helps you feel relaxed. Maybe do some stretches. I personally love taking a long walk *while* listening to music or a fun podcast. One of my favorite podcasts is *Lore*, hosted by Aaron Mahnke. A song you could listen to is "Here Comes a Thought" from the cartoon *Steven Universe*, which focuses on how to let go of your anxiety.

3 **Talk to someone.** Sometimes the best thing you can do is talk to someone you trust about how you feel. Talking things out can make you feel a lot better. And if you'd like to chat with someone who's a pro at talking to people, consider a therapist—a trained professional whose job is to help you work through how you feel and improve your mental health. Therapy can give you all sorts of tools to help soothe your anxiety and stress while teaching you how to become a better version of your already awesome self!

So that's how you put the *chill* in *Chilling with Ghosts*—see what I did there? Sorry, couldn't resist. Anyway, it's about time we moved onto the next chapter . . . the history of ghosts!

"Wait," you might be saying, "that's it? No actual busting happened! All we did was talk about . . . talking!" You're right. When it comes to ghosts, the best thing you can do for them is help them move on peacefully. Sure, you could make like the Ghostbusters and break out the proton pack, but when dealing with the supernatural, you want to be cautious and respectful. If you ever ran into a ghost, you'd want to show them the respect you would show to any other person. At the end of the day, the best way to bust a ghost is to *not* bust a ghost. Just talk to them, if that's possible, or leave them alone.

We covered the basics of ghost lore, and now we've covered how to deal with ghosts. If you're tired, take a moment to rest, or maybe do a little dance break to your favorite spooky tune. If you're ready to keep reading, let's go—we're about to hit the history books!

DIY Ectoslime

Are you curious what ectoplasm, as seen in movies like *Ghostbusters*, feels like? You're in luck! At Totally Factual Field Guide to the Supernatural HQ we have the perfect recipe to make your very own ectoplasm slime. (No ghosts were harmed in the making of this ectoslime. In fact, no ghosts were involved at all! That would've been super weird: "Hey, ghost friend, can I have some of your ectoplasm?" So awkward.) WARNING: This should be obvious, but don't eat it! Ectoslime is definitely not edible!

MATERIALS

1 bottle white or clear nontoxic liquid glue

A disposable or easily washable bowl (to pour glue into)

1 teaspoon baking soda

Food coloring (green, or any color you like!)

A wooden ice-pop stick or something to stir with

A timer or clock

1–2 teaspoons contact lens solution (or liquid dish soap), or more as needed

BONUS: Want to take your ectoslime to the next level?
Make it extra spooky by adding googly eyes or plastic spiders!

INSTRUCTIONS

1 Dump the entire bottle of glue into a bowl. (It's best to use a disposable or easily washable bowl—things are going to get messy! A clear bowl will be great for seeing the colors of your ectoslime.)

2 Add the baking soda.

3 Carefully add just a couple of drops of food coloring. Remember, a little goes a long way! If you don't get the color you want, you can add more in step 5.

4 Stir everything up with the ice-pop stick. Keep stirring for a good 2 minutes. (The timer or clock helps with this.)

5 After mixing for 2 minutes, add the contact lens solution. Start with 1 or 2 teaspoons. (If using liquid dish soap, add it slowly.) If the color of the mixture isn't dark enough, add another drop or 2 of food coloring.

6 Mix everything again, using your hands this time, until the slime doesn't stick to your fingers. This may take 5 to 10 minutes, but just keep going. If your slime sticks to your fingers, add 1 more teaspoon of contact lens solution and mix it in.

7 Once your ectoslime is a consistency that you like, take it out of the bowl to play with.

Chapter 3

PHANTOMS OF THE PAST

Within this temporal body.... There resides a spirit which, for lack of an adequate name, I think of as windblown.

—Matsuo Bashō

Let's head all the way back to ancient times to check out what ancient mythology had to say about ghosts. From there, we'll step forward in time to learn how different cultures view ghosts today. Ghosts are a major part of just about every culture. Why is that? The answer has to do with . . . death.

DEATH?!

Yes, death. Let's talk about it. Death is a natural and inevitable occurrence. As Benjamin Franklin once wrote, "nothing can be said to be certain, except death and taxes." You may know someone who has passed away and feel sadness about losing them. But even though that person is no longer around, they still live on in your memories and your heart. If you ever feel alone or scared about death, it's okay. Just talk about it with someone you love and trust!

Throughout history, people have tried to understand death using science, philosophy, religion, and more. And the conclusions people came to, whether accurate or not, influence how we understand death and loss today. These conclusions also influence how we think about the human soul, our memories of the past, and, yes, ghosts.

According to Science

Thanatology is the study of death and loss. This field examines various aspects of death, including how death affects you psychologically, medically, and spiritually. It also explores ways to help people cope with grief. If you've ever experienced loss and need to talk to someone, there are plenty of fantastic and skilled therapists and grief counselors out there. There are also some books that may help you, including: *A Kids Book About Grief* by Brennan C. Wood, *How I Feel: Grief Journal for Kids* by Mia Roldan, and *Welcome to the Grief Club* by Janine Kwoh.

So what exactly did people think about death and the afterlife in ancient times? Let's venture back in time to get a glimpse of life—and death—back in the old days.

DEATH, BURIALS, AND THE AFTERLIFE IN ANCIENT TIMES

There's no better place to start our journey through the past than Mesopotamia! From there, we'll head to ancient Egypt and ancient Greece.

Ancient Mesopotamia

Mesopotamia lies within the region of southwest Asia, between the Tigris and Euphrates Rivers. *Mesopotamia* is Greek for "the land between the rivers," and some of the world's first human civilizations were located here, dating back to the Stone Age! (Fred Flintstone, is that you?) Ancient Mesopotamia saw quite a few major achievements, including the invention of cuneiform, the written version of the Sumerian language. Cuneiform was written with a stylus on slabs of wet clay. (Imagine having to write on clay instead of using pencil and paper! Doing your homework would take forever.) Today, this region is part of the Middle East and home to countries such as Iraq, Iran, Turkey, Syria, and Kuwait.

In ancient Mesopotamian culture, the dead were often buried underground or near the family home. Kinda weird, right? But it wasn't considered weird at the time! It actually made a lot of sense, because family members could easily maintain the grave without having to travel far. This wasn't true for everyone, though; some people, like deceased royalty, were buried in chambers made of brick or stone. They were buried with objects that were closely associated with them or meant to be carried into the afterlife. A proper burial was considered incredibly important—people believed that the dead would come back as ghosts if they weren't correctly laid to rest!

Ancient Egypt

The ancient Egyptians believed in immortality and thought that a person's soul would eventually return to their body. If someone with high social status, like royalty, passed away, they were mummified immediately after death. Their body was preserved inside linen wraps and placed within a tomb. (Pets, such as cats, dogs, and birds, were also mummified!) Everyday folks, however, weren't mummified; they were simply buried underground.

After death, the Egyptians was believed that you went to the Hall of Truth, where your soul would be judged by forty-two judges and Osiris, the god of the dead and the afterlife. To judge you, they would weigh your heart against the feather of truth, a feather used to determine if your soul deserved to move on to the afterlife. If your

heart was heavier than the feather, your soul would be fed to the god Amenti. If your heart was lighter than the feather, then you headed to the A'Aru, also known as the Field of Reeds, a place that resembled where the deceased lived on earth. However, some souls had reason to return to the world of the living, maybe because their body hadn't been buried properly or because they had something to atone for. These souls were considered ghosts.

So how did mummification work? Starting around 2400 BCE, mummification was used in ancient Egypt to preserve bodies. It was a long and involved process:

1. First, the body was cleansed and embalmed with palm wine and water from the Nile River to keep it from decaying.

2. Next, the brain was removed with a large hook. Then the internal organs, stomach, lungs, and other stuff on the inside were also removed and embalmed. All of that went into designated porcelain or limestone jars called canopic jars. Each jar held a specific organ.

3. The body was dried out with a type of salt known as natron salt and left outside for forty days to continue the dehydration process.

4. After forty days, the body was filled with straw, linen, and sand.

5. Once the body was blessed, the body was wrapped in linen. Special makeup and a mask were placed on the body, along with plenty of amulets.

Can you believe that morticians, the people who prepare and care for bodies after death, still use some of these processes today? Science might seem like something that only exists in the modern day, but in fact, scientific progress—including how to preserve a body—is built on research and knowledge from the past!

Ancient Greece

In ancient Greece, mythology played a vital role in how people lived their lives. They believed that when someone died, it was important to honor them. They put carved stones over burial sites to let passersby know who the deceased was.

People would also place a coin in the deceased's mouth. According to Greek mythology, the spirits of the dead were greeted by the god of peaceful death, Thanatos. Then the dead would travel to the underworld, or Hades, via the River Styx. To get across this river, the dead would need to pay Charon, the ferryman, with their coin.

Read All About It

Hades wasn't just the name of the underworld in Greek mythology. Hades was also the name of the king of the underworld and the god of death (not to be confused with Thanatos, the god of peaceful death). You might know Hades from the legend of Hades and Persephone, or even from the *Hades* video game released in 2020. Another denizen of the underworld? Cerberus, the three-headed dog who guards its gates!

Spirits were meant to stick around in the underworld, but of course, there were exceptions. In Greek mythology, there were three types of spirits that would sneak off to become ghosts:

1 **Ataphoi:** Souls who weren't buried with the correct rituals.

2 **Aōroi:** Souls who died prematurely—that is, too early.

3 **Biaiothanatoi:** Souls who were the victims of violence, such as soldiers who died during war.

You might have noticed a running theme among these various cultures; proper burial and respect for the dead was incredibly important during ancient times. And that still holds true today, even if our burial practices look pretty different.

Read All About It

According to Greek mythology, Hecate (or Hekate) is the goddess of magic, crossroads, graves, night, and . . . *ghosts*! Hecate is typically depicted holding two burning torches. She is also depicted standing back-to-back with three other versions of herself, which symbolizes coming to a crossroad.

GOING GHOST IN THE MIDDLE AGES

European beliefs about death, the afterlife, and ghosts in the medieval era were shaped largely by the Catholic church.

For a little context, the Middle Ages took place in Europe between 500 CE to 1500 CE—right after Roman Empire fell until the Renaissance was just starting. During that time, many people were suffering from disease, famine, and war. With death and disease running rampant, people worried about whether their souls would make it into heaven.

At first, ghosts were considered demonic apparitions and not actually the spirits of the deceased. Later on, the Catholic church (reluctantly) embraced ghosts, claiming that they were souls trapped in purgatory, a place where souls atoned for their sins before being admitted to heaven. These souls were said to come back to haunt the living for a variety of reasons, such as having unfinished business, not having had a chance to say goodbye, or not having been buried incorrectly. Ghosts would appear to ask relatives for prayers or pass messages to the living.

Ye Olde History

Ah-CHOO! Why do people say "bless you" when someone sneezes? Back when Rome was suffering from the bubonic plague, Pope Gregory I thought that people should start saying "God bless you" after someone sneezed. It was thought this would protect the sneezer from dying and prevent their soul from being sneezed out of their body! Another common superstitious practice is holding your breath when you go past a cemetery. The idea is that you don't want to disturb the ghosts or accidentally breathe one in.

GHOSTS ON HOLIDAY

Many holidays, superstitions, and cultural practices have their roots in long-established traditions and ancient history. Did you know there are several holidays associated with ghosts? Here are a few.

The Hungry Ghost Festival

Ever heard of the Gregorian calendar? That's the calendar that you most likely follow in your daily life. This calendar is based on the earth's path around the sun. The calendar based on the moon's phases is known as the lunar calendar. During the seventh month of the lunar calendar, many countries in Asia celebrate the Hungry Ghost Festival or something similar to it. The seventh month is known as Ghost Month, and the festival takes place on the fifteenth day of that month.

The festival is a cultural and religious event when the spirits of deceased ancestors, along with other ghosts and spirits, return to the land of the living. During Ghost Month, people present food offerings to their ancestors, light lanterns, and burn fake money (known as "hell money") and incense to pay their respects. Lanterns are also floated down a river.

During Ghost Month, it's advised to avoid:

- **Getting married:** Good luck is important when tying the knot. Getting married during Ghost Month is bad luck and might result in unwanted guests of the spectral kind.
- **Hanging your clothes outside at night:** It's said that a spirit might steal a piece of your clothing to wear. Yikes!
- **Shaving your legs:** According to an old Chinese proverb, your leg hair can defend against ghosts.

- **Whistling to yourself:** Ghosts are drawn to the sound of whistling, which is certainly attention-grabbing.
- **Staying out late:** Ghosts are thought to be strongest at night, so staying out past sunset is not the safest thing to do during Ghost Month. Head home early . . . or beware!

Day of the Dead

Day of the Dead, or Día de los Muertos, is a Mexican holiday celebrating life and death. It takes place on November 1 and 2 of every year and is observed primarily in Mexico but also celebrated in countries such as the Philippines, Guatemala, Ecuador, El Salvador, Brazil, and Haiti. On these days, there is dancing, music, and food, such as pan de muerto, a traditional sweet bread coated in sugar. Families build altars in their homes dedicated to the deceased, and colorful, decorated sugar skulls are placed upon them as offerings. Skulls and skeletons are a big part of Day of the Dead. They remind people that death is a part of life and that the two are intertwined.

Halloween

You might think Halloween, also known as All Hallows' Eve, is all about trick-or-treating, but it actually has ghostly beginnings. Its history starts with the Celtic festival of Samhain. Samhain marked both the end of the harvest season and when the Celts believed that souls of the dead passed through the land of the living. To shoo ghosts away, people wore masks and set fires to frighten them. Much later, Pope Boniface IV declared November 1, a.k.a. Samhain, to be All Saints' Day. The day before, October 31, is considered the hallowed eve of All Saints' Day. (Get it? See what they did there?)

Nowadays, celebrating Halloween means throwing on a costume and trick-or-treating for candy. What have I dressed up as? Hmm, let's see! Once I dressed up as a banshee from the game Dungeons and Dragons, and another time, I dressed up as the teenage witch Rochelle from the 1996 movie *The Craft*.

We've talked about so much in this chapter, haven't we? Death, mythology, history, and holidays. In the next chapter, we're going to explore the world of ghost stories. But first . . . a tasty treat!

Haunted Graveyard Parfait

In the mood for a spooky yet delicious treat? I have just the thing!

INGREDIENTS

4 to 5 chocolate sandwich cookies

1 pint strawberries

1 bar chocolate (about 1.5 ounces)

24 ounces Greek yogurt or regular yogurt

Gummy worms

¼ cup granola

Marshmallows

INSTRUCTIONS

1 Take the chocolate sandwich cookies, drop them in a large bowl, and crush them up using your hands or spoon. Crush them just enough to create a loose crumble. Set aside.

2 Rinse the strawberries and pat them dry. With the help of an adult, cut off the green stem and cut the berries into small pieces; set aside. Break the chocolate bar into pieces, place them in a small bowl, and set aside.

3 Add 1 cup of yogurt to a tall clear glass (or a mug or a bowl). Use the back of a spoon to smooth out the yogurt in an even layer.

4 Sprinkle some of the crushed cookies on top of the yogurt to create a layer of cookies.

5 Continue alternating between layering yogurt and cookies. Throw in some gummy worms and granola wherever you see fit! Just be sure to leave some room on the top.

6 Finish your parfait with a thin layer of yogurt and a final sprinkling of cookies. This is the dirt for your graveyard!

7 Now, it's time to decorate! Add the strawberries, throw in more gummy worms, and stick in a few chunks of chocolate. Make sure those chocolate pieces are standing upright—those are your tombstones! Finally, place a few marshmallow ghosts around the tombstones. Happy eating!

Chapter 4

DEAD MEN TELL NO TALES

We need ghost
stories because we,
in fact, are the ghosts.

—Stephen King,
Danse Macabre

Tired from time traveling and chilling with ghosts? Take a seat! Let's toast some s'mores because tonight, we're getting into ghost stories of all kinds. I'm talking spooky ghost stories you tell around a campfire and legendary ghosts that haunt the pages of classic literature. Ghost stories were popular in the past, and they're still popular today! Here's a question for you to chew on: just why exactly are ghost stories so popular?

LONG, LONG AGO LITERATURE

In Chapter 3, we talked about ghosts that appeared in ancient mythology and legends. But ghosts have haunted just about every kind of fiction from the dawn of time, ranging from oral storytelling to written novels and plays performed on stage. Just as our history and our past shape how we understand our present, old ghost stories shape how we perceive ghosts in our modern-day lives. How about we take a look at some of these old ghost stories?

The Odyssey

The Odyssey is an epic poem written around the eighth century BCE. *Poem* doesn't mean it was short—it spanned twenty-four books! *The Odyssey* tells the long journey (which is what *odyssey* means) of the Greek hero Odysseus. At the start of the story, Odysseus is leaving Troy after the ten-year Trojan war. He heads home to Ithaca, but his journey isn't smooth sailing. The epic poem covers the ten (yes, ten!) years it takes him to get home. Talk about taking the scenic route!

During Odysseus's never-ending road trip, he runs into all kinds of monsters, gods, and powerful beings—including an enchantress named Circe who can turn men into pigs, a one-eyed Cyclops, and Sirens who lure sailors to their doom with beautiful singing.

In Book 11, Odysseus heads to the Land of the Dead to speak with the seer Teiresias about going home. There, he encounters his old crewmate Elpenor, who has died an untimely death. Elpenor asks Odysseus to bring his body back to Aeaea to give it a proper burial.

Odysseus also speaks with his deceased mother and two other heroes named Agamemnon and Achilles. Achilles asks after his son, and Odysseus reassures him that Achilles's son is also a brave hero.

Throughout Odysseus's journey to the underworld, we meet ghosts who long for their loved ones, yearn to complete their unfinished business, and worry about their legacy.

Read All About It

Does the phrase *Achilles' heel* sound familiar? In Greek mythology, Achilles was invulnerable everywhere except his heel, which is where his mom had held him when she dunked him in the River Styx to give him the power of invulnerability.

Tales as Old as Time

The Odyssey isn't the only ancient tale that features ghosts. The spooky and the spectral appear in countless ancient myths, legends, and story collections. Other epics and classic works of literature with ghosts include:

- *Epic of Gilgamesh*: This epic poem dates back to 2100 BCE, but a later version was compiled by a priest and scholar named Sîn-lēqi-unninni. The epic tells the story of King Gilgamesh, who angers the gods and loses his companion Enkidu. He then embarks on a journey to seek immortality.

- *One Thousand and One Nights* (or *Arabian Nights*): From the late 1200s CE, this Middle Eastern collection of many stories from different genres includes a framing device in which a woman named Scheherazade is telling these stories to her husband to keep him from executing her. One story depicts a house haunted by a jinn, or a shape-shifting spirit. The tale of Aladdin's lamp was added to this collection much later, in 1704!

- *Eyrbyggja saga* (Saga of the People of Eyri): This Icelandic saga written in the thirteenth century CE spans many generations, giving us a literary epic of feuding families, supernatural hauntings, and more!

- *The Tale of Genji:* Written by Murasaki Shikibu in the eleventh century CE, *The Tale of Genji* is considered one of the first novels ever written! This work tells the story of the emperor's son, a handsome man named Hikaru Genji, and all his romantic troubles. In one chapter, he falls in love with a beautiful woman named Yugao—but she is killed by the angry spirit of Genji's ex, a woman named Lady Rokujo.

As you can see, people have been telling ghostly stories since, well, forever! Let's look at a few more classics that are just a tiny bit more recent . . .

All the World's a Stage

Born in Stratford-upon-Avon, England, in 1564, William Shakespeare needs no introduction—but I'm giving him one anyway! He was a renowned poet and playwright who wrote 154 sonnets, 39 plays, and 3 narrative poems. Here to talk to us about the ghosts in his most famous works is the Bard of Avon himself. Or, at least, his ghost.

GUIDE: Hey there, Willy! Can I call you Willy?

SHAKESPEARE: You most certainly cannot. Where am I?

GUIDE: Don't you worry about that, Willy. We've summoned your ghost to tell us all about your fictional ghosts.

SHAKESPEARE: I'm an apparition?! Oh no! That cannot be!

GUIDE: Chill, Willy. Now we've only got a few minutes to chat, so let's get down to it. Tell me about your top two ghosts.

SHAKESPEARE: Ah! Yes. I believe my most infamous ghosts appear in *The Tragedy of Hamlet, Prince of Denmark* and *The Tragedy of Macbeth*.

GUIDE: So, spill. What's the deal with these ghosts?

SHAKESPEARE: *The Tragedy of Hamlet, Prince of Denmark* is the tale of a young prince who returns home to discover that his dear father hath passed beyond the mortal veil. Claudius, his dastardly uncle, marries Hamlet's mother and becomes the new king of Denmark. On a cold night, Hamlet is called to approach his father, who appears to him as a ghost!

GUIDE: And what does Hamlet Senior want?

SHAKESPEARE: The elder Hamlet desires sweet, sweet revenge against his brother, Claudius, who murdered him! But the path to vengeance hath never runneth smooth . . . eth. Throughout my play, Prince Hamlet does indeed struggle to act. His dilemma is captured by his famous soliloquy . . . To be!

GUIDE: Ooh! I know this one. "Or not to be!"

SHAKESPEARE: Yes, yes! That is the question! You know it well.

GUIDE: Yeah, they teach *Hamlet* in high school.

SHAKESPARE: What is this high school you speak of?

GUIDE: It's, like, school. For teens? Never mind. What about the ghost in *Macbeth*?

SHAKESPEARE: Ah, Banquo. Long story short, a Scottish general named Macbeth encounters three terrible witches on a rainy heath. The hags spell Macbeth's downfall! They tell him that he is destined to become Thane of Cawdor and, later, the king! When he does indeed become Thane of Cawdor . . .

GUIDE: Let me guess, Macbeth gets power hungry.

SHAKESPEARE: Aye. He and his wife, Lady Macbeth, decide to make the final prophecy come true . . . through murder most foul! Macbeth stabs King Banquo, killing him.

GUIDE: But that's not the end of the story.

SHAKESPEARE: No. Macbeth is visited by the ghost of King Banquo not once, not twice, but three times! Seeing the ghost, Macbeth is wracked by guilt and fear over what he has done. He fails to hold on to power and, well . . . many people die.

GUIDE: And on that bummer note, that's all the time we have with Willy Shakes. Oh, one more thing. Did you know that your play *Hamlet* kind of inspired *The Lion King*?

SHAKESPEARE: Pardon? What is this king of lions you speak of?

GUIDE: So there's this lion called Mufasa, and he has an evil brother named Scar, and then . . . never mind. You should really get back to your eternal rest. Goodbye, Willy Shakes!

MUCH ADO ABOUT SHAKESPEARE

Not only did William Shakespeare write many world-famous plays and introduce several spine-chilling fictional ghosts to the world, but he also coined quite a few words: *bandit, lonely, bump, auspicious,* and *road,* to name just a few. The fun thing about language is that it's always changing—and during his day, Shakespeare was part of that change! What are some new words that have been invented this year? Do you have any favorites? Have you ever tried to coin a new word?

Read All About It

Actors never, ever say the name of *Macbeth* in a theater. Instead, they call it "the Scottish play." Legend has it that speaking the name *Macbeth* in a theater will result in terrible misfortune! Incidents that back up this claim include actors experiencing injuries, burns, and bad performances.

A NOT-SO-SLEEPY LEGEND

Another ghost story to send a shiver down your spine is "The Legend of Sleepy Hollow." First published in 1819 by the American writer Washington Irving, this haunting tale went on to inspire many films and TV shows, along with plays and even songs! Read on to find out what this short story is all about.

Out-of-Town Man Disappears from Sleepy Hollow, Locals Blame Headless Horseman

It was an ordinary balmy autumn day in the countryside town of Sleepy Hollow. But that night, schoolmaster Ichabod Crane went missing.

According to one Diedrich Knickerbocker, Crane was last seen leaving a party attended by some of Sleepy Hollow's finest personages, including the handsome Abraham "Brom Bones" Van Brunt and the beautiful Katrina Van Tassel. As Crane approached a bridge, the hoofbeats of a horse sounded in the night.

"I heard it. Crane tried calling out to the horse rider behind him. He yelled, 'Hello! Hello!' but whoever it was, he just kept racing toward Crane!" said Knickerbocker, a longtime resident of Sleepy Hollow.

Knickerbocker continued, "Crane turned around, but it was too late. This terrible rider was upon him. And he was headless! Carrying what looked like a pumpkin in his lap."

According to Knickerbocker, this mysterious headless rider threw the pumpkin at Crane, knocking Crane off his own horse. The following morning, Crane's horse was found back at home, but Crane was nowhere to be seen. He had vanished into the night.

Locals have not given up on the hope of finding the schoolmaster, but life has gone on in the meantime. Katrina Van Tassel and Abraham Van Brunt have wed. When this paper asked for a comment about Crane, Van Brunt simply laughed.

Terrifying Tales

The *Flying Dutchman* is the name of a ship that never made it safely back to port, doomed to continue sailing the high seas forever as an eerie apparition and an omen of bad luck. In the Nickelodeon cartoon *SpongeBob SquarePants*, the Flying Dutchman is not a ship but a neon-green ghost pirate!

POE THE POET

Of course, we can't talk about ghastly storytelling without talking about Edgar Allan Poe! Born in Boston, Massachusetts, on January 19, 1809, he was an American poet, author, and editor. His writing often explored themes such as death and grief, and he wrote quite a few works of gothic horror.

Read All About It

Gothic horror, a.k.a. gothic fiction, is a type of fiction that is characterized by its haunting tone and bleak setting. Gothic fiction often features the supernatural, whether that's ghosts, vampires, or just incredibly spooky vibes.

I could go on forever talking about my favorite works by Edgar Allan Poe, but I'll just cover a few of his biggest hits. There's "The Tell-Tale Heart," a story about . . . well, I'm not going to tell you.

Just read it! It's short and downright spine-chilling. Another famous Poe story that's scarily fun and worth checking out is "The Cask of Amontillado." This is one of his many stories that feature murder most foul. And finally, we can't forget about "The Fall of the House of Usher," a terrifying work of gothic fiction.

Poe's most famous poetry includes the poems "Annabel Lee," "Lenore," and "The Raven." That last one features a man sitting alone mourning for someone he lost, when he's visited by a raven. In the past, ravens were sometimes considered symbols of bad luck and death. (Ravens were also depicted as prophetic and linked to the spiritual world. Ravens contain multitudes!) So what does the raven say to this man again and again? Quoth the Raven "Nevermore."

Poe was an inspiration to many other authors, including the science fiction writer H. G. Wells (author of *The War of the Worlds*) and Sir Arthur Conan Doyle (the creator of Sherlock Holmes!). Edgar Allan Poe passed away on October 7, 1849, leaving behind a legacy of short stories and poems that live on forevermore.

According to Science

Ravens and crows might look similar, but they're totally distinct birds! *Corvus corax*, or the common raven, tends to be larger than *Corvus brachyrhynchos*, or the American crow. In fact, a crow weighs half as much as a raven! A few other ways to tell these two guys apart: The raven's tail feather formation is more pointed, whereas the crow's tail feathers look like a fan when they're spread out. A raven's beak is larger than a crow's, and a little bit curved. A crow typically makes a cawing noise, whereas ravens sort of croak.

TELLING TALL TALES

Gather round, let me tell you a ghost story that was once told to me . . .

Two teen girls are having a sleepover and talk about what to do for the night. One mentions hearing about a game that's all the rage—you stand in front of a mirror and summon a ghost. Later that night, the girls gather in the bathroom. They dim the lights, set a candle between them, and say the following words:

Bloody Mary

Bloody Mary

Bloody Mary

Just as they say the words for the third time, the two girls let out a sigh of relief. Whew! Nothing happened. But when the girls look in the mirror, they're not alone. They see a woman with blood dripping down her head. She slowly grins at them, revealing bloody teeth. The girls scream and scream in terror. The woman reaches through the mirror, reaching for the two girls . . . and soon, their screams are heard no more.

Boo! That's the terrifying tale of Bloody Mary. You may have heard this story before, and maybe the version you heard is different. That's the thing about ghost stories and urban legends—they often shift and change with each telling.

In addition to retelling ghost stories you've heard, you can also write your own! Kim Newman, a film critic and horror novelist, writes that there are five types of ghost stories: regular ghost stories that portray a standard ghost encounter, funny ghost stories (*Ghostbusters* is a great example of this), sentimental ghost stories about lost loved ones, scary ghost stories that fit right in with horror movies, and fake ghost stories in which the ghost isn't really a ghost—like in the Scooby-Doo cartoon! What kind of ghost story appeals to you?

Here's how to write a ghost story:

① Find out what scares you. The best kind of story is the kind that you, the storyteller, enjoy! Knowing what scares you will help you decide what to include in your ghost story.

② Pick the type of ghost story you'd like to tell. Do you want to make people laugh with a funny story? Or are you ready to scare everyone's socks off with a frightening tale?

③ Who is your ghost? Take time to brainstorm your ghost's backstory. Why did they die? Do they have unfinished business?

④ Build your setting and pick your characters. Where does this story take place? Who in your story gets haunted? What kind of characters would make your story interesting? Think about the atmosphere you want your story to have.

⑤ Start outlining. Once you have a general idea of what you want in your ghost story, try building your story! You'll be surprised by what you come up with as you write. And don't worry, it doesn't have to be perfect the first time. But getting your words out is the first step!

The Ultimate Ghost Story

Let's play a game! Spoiler alert: it's a storytelling game. You'll need a six-sided die. If you don't have one, you can google "six-sided die" and find a website where you can use a virtual one! For each of the six categories below, roll the die to select ONE item from the category. Once you have all your selections, you'll write a story that includes them. (I've included an example story on page 92 to show you how it works.)

GHOST

1. Residual ghost
2. Poltergeist
3. Orb
4. Mist
5. Funnel ghost
6. Ghost pet

HAUNTED PLACE

1. Mansion
2. School
3. Forest
4. Graveyard
5. Museum
6. Bathroom

FIRST HAUNTING INCIDENT

1. Knock on a door
2. The sound of whispering, laughter, or talking
3. Cold spots
4. Lights flickering on and off
5. Strange smells emanating from nowhere
6. Trail of neon-green ectoplasm

SECOND HAUNTING INCIDENT

1. Someone says "Heeeeeeere's ghostie!"
2. Someone feels like they're being watched and no one is there
3. Shadows against the wall look eerily human
4. A figure walks through a wall like it's not there
5. Objects go missing or move spontaneously
6. Pet refuses to enter a particular room or place

GHOST-BUSTING EQUIPMENT

1. Phone
2. Thermometer
3. Notebook
4. Proton pack
5. EMF meter
6. Snack

GHOST BE GONE

1. Talk to the ghost
2. Use every tool in the Ghastly Ghostly Tool Kit (page 42)
3. Challenge the ghost to a dance-off
4. Trap the ghost
5. Politely ask the ghost to go away
6. Ghost the ghost—just ignore them!

Here's my story:

Years ago, I went hiking alone. At night, I found shelter in an abandoned cabin in the **forest**. As I started to fall asleep, I heard a **knock on the door**. The knocking grew louder and louder, and then suddenly stopped. I ventured out of the bedroom, and at first, I saw nothing. But then I glimpsed a **shadow on the wall** starting to writhe and twist! A howling wind filled the cabin, knocking over candlesticks and sending plates crashing to the ground. It was then I realized that I was facing a **poltergeist**! I wanted to run, to flee and never look back, but I knew I wouldn't be safe if I ran.

My hands shaking, I took out a **notebook** from my knapsack and wrote a message: "What do you want? How can I help you?" The shadowy figure extended a finger and traced a word, spelling "hungry." I reached into my **Ghastly Ghostly Tool Kit** and poured everything on the table . . . and out tumbled a granola bar and a box of ghost-shaped sugar cookies! The darkness flared, and the snacks disappeared. The poltergeist was nowhere to be seen, and all was well . . . at least, for the time being.

Chapter 5

HAUNTED HOUSES AND SPOOKY SPOTS

Silence lay steadily against the wood and stone of Hill House, and whatever walked there, walked alone.

—Shirley Jackson, *The Haunting of Hill House*

Ghosts are said to linger in countless places, ranging from a regular house to a grand mansion or, as you read in the last chapter, even a ship. Why do ghosts haunt these spots? Most likely because they have some kind of connection or tie to that place. Maybe a certain diner is a ghost's favorite place to get waffles. Or maybe a specific graveyard spot is a ghost's final resting place. Whatever the reason may be, haunted places exist all over the world. In this chapter we're going to read about a few of them.

La Isla de las Muñecas

Imagine a small island with more than two hundred dolls hanging from trees and fences. It's a terrifying thought! That's what you would encounter on La Isla de las Muñecas, the Island of the Dolls.

LOCATION: Parque Ecológico de Xochimilco, Mexico

BACKSTORY: A man named Don Julián Santana Barrera was finishing up a day's work, and as he crossed the lake, he noticed something in the water. Sadly, he found a little girl who had drowned in the lake and, next to her, a doll. Hoping the little girl's spirit would find peace in the afterlife, Julián hung up the doll in a tree. After that, whenever he found a doll, he brought it back to the island and hung it up to honor the girl. Julián became the unspoken caretaker of the island, keeping the island filled with dolls, until he passed away in 2001.

HOW HAUNTED IS IT?: Locals have reported hearing the dolls whispering to one another or claimed to have seen the dolls open their eyes.

Winchester Mystery House

In 1886, Sarah Winchester started a renovation project in her sprawling Victorian-style mansion. The renovations continued for thirty-six years and stopped only when Sarah passed away in 1922.

LOCATION: San Jose, California

BACKSTORY: In 1862, Sarah Lockwood Pardee married William Winchester, the heir to the Winchester Repeating Arms Company, a firearms company that manufactured the Winchester Rifle, known as the "Gun of the West." Even though business was booming, tragedy struck the Winchester family when their infant daughter Annie passed away. Then in 1881, William died of tuberculosis. From that point, Sarah Winchester's story is a bit of mystery. According to legend, after her husband died, Sarah consulted a medium, who told her that the spirits killed by Winchester rifles were haunting her. In order to appease these spirits, the medium told Sarah she must build a house for the spirits and that construction could not stop until the ghosts were happy. After this, Sarah moved to the West Coast, purchased an eight-bedroom farmhouse, and began transforming it into a sprawling mansion. At least, that's the story. We don't truly know Sarah's motivations for building her house the way she did. Her story has likely been sensationalized to fit into a haunting narrative.

HOW HAUNTED IS IT?: Visitors to the Winchester Mystery House and members of its staff have claimed that the house is haunted. A ghost is said to have been seen pushing a wheelbarrow filled with coal to a fireplace. Mysterious sighs and shadowy figures have also been reported.

Stanley Hotel

Ever heard of the novelist Stephen King? The hotel in his 1977 horror novel *The Shining* is inspired by this real-life hotel.

LOCATION: Estes Park, Colorado

BACKSTORY: In 1903, an inventor named Freelan Oscar Stanley was suffering from tuberculosis. He was told the best way to treat the illness was to breathe as much fresh air as possible. (This is not how you treat tuberculosis.) He and his wife, Flora, packed their things and moved to the Rocky Mountains. Freelan loved the area so much that he decided to turn the town of Estes Park into a resort town, and in 1909, Freelan and Flora built the Stanley Hotel there. Initially the hotel was flourishing, but after 1940, the hotel started to fail and spooky legends about the hotel started to circulate . . .

HOW HAUNTED IS IT?: Room 2017 is said to be haunted by the late housekeeper of the hotel (this was where Stephen King and his wife stayed when they visited in 1974). And legend has it that Flora can be heard playing at the piano at night in the hotel's concert hall. The Stanley Hotel is also said to contain a spot called "The Vortex," an area where ghosts enter and leave the hotel.

Read All About It

Stephen King has been dubbed "The King of Horror" by fans of his books and short stories and film adaptations of his work. King's first novel, *Carrie*, was published in 1974. Over the decades, King has written more than 60 books and 200 short stories. If you're curious about his books, you can find them at your local library or bookstore—but be warned, you might not sleep for days!

Catacombs of Paris

Are you brave enough to wander around a tunnel lined with bones? If you think you've got the stomach for it, add the Catacombs of Paris to your itinerary if you ever visit France!

LOCATION: Paris, France

BACKSTORY: During the eighteenth century, the city of Paris was packed with people—both the living and the dead! With no space to bury the dead, the city looked underground. Beneath the streets were old quarries, or mines, that weren't being used. Those underground spaces were converted to what we now know as the Catacombs of Paris. More than six million skeletons reside there. When you enter, there is a large stone in the passageway stating ARRÊTE! C'EST ICI L'EMPIRE DE LA MORT, meaning "Stop! This is the empire of death." As of 2020, a small portion of the catacombs is open to visitors.

HOW HAUNTED IS IT?: Legends claim that on the streets of Paris, you can hear whispers from beneath your feet. Once you descend into the catacombs, you might even hear louder whispers coming from the walls, which are said to come alive at night.

Queen Mary

The ship known as *Queen Mary* has plenty of stories to tell!

....

LOCATION: Long Beach, California

....

BACKSTORY: RMS *Queen Mary* has had a spectacular and haunting history. Launched in 1934, this beautiful luxury liner was outfitted with a grand ballroom, swimming pools, and more. But it did not stay a luxury liner for long. During World War II, the *Queen Mary* was commandeered to assist with transporting Australian troops and painted gray, earning it the nickname "the Grey Ghost." By 1947, the ship returned to shore and was renamed the *Queen Mary*.

....

HOW HAUNTED IS IT?: A number of tragedies have contributed to the ship's reputation, and most have happened in Stateroom B340, the most haunted room on the ship. In 1966, a passenger woke after a long night to find a man standing at the end of her bed. When help arrived, the man was nowhere to be found . . . Some believe that this was the ghost of a passenger named Walter J. Adamson, who passed away in that same room in 1948.

According to Science

What happens to your body when you experience fear? A couple of things! When we're scared, the sensation of fear triggers our fight-or-flight response. Stress hormones such as adrenaline are released, your heart may start to beat faster, your blood pressure may rise, and your breathing might speed up, too.

All these terrifying tales got me thinking: why do people like haunted houses anyway? To answer that, we need to think about the emotion of fear.

First of all, there is nothing wrong with fear or being scared. We experience fear when our minds recognize something as a threat or danger—and that fear can keep us safe! But for some people—maybe even you—fear can also be cathartic, thrilling, or just plain fun. Horror movies, roller coasters, and haunted houses are popular for a reason, after all. So where do you stand on fear? Is it something you avoid at all costs, or something you enjoy facing down?

If you love a good fright and know others who do, too, we've got just the thing! Have you ever considered hosting your very own haunted house? Keep reading to find out how you can do just that.

Make Your Own Haunted House

Looking for something spooky and fun to do? Here's how to plan your own haunted house.

1. **Recruit your friends and family to help!** If they're up for it, ask them what they'd like to assist with. Could they play a spooky ghost, help with decor, or spread the word about the haunted house?

2. **Plan how you'll make your house feel haunted.** A haunted house is all about spooky vibes, spooky decorations, spooky music, spooky scares, and spooky snacks! A few things you'll want to do:

   - Sketch out a map of your home and each of the rooms, and figure out what can go where. Should a zombie jump out of your bathroom? Will there be a ghost wailing in the kitchen?
   - Plan out roles and scary costumes for your actors.
   - Make a list of spooky decorations and start crafting! Pro tip: you can buy decorations at your local craft store or party supply store.
   - Put together a playlist of spooky tunes.
   - Make a safety plan. You'll want to know what to do if emergencies pop up. Where are the exits? Do you have back-up flashlights and bottled water? Where is your first-aid kit?

3. **Put your plan into action!** Choose the day your haunted house will open, and get to work!

4 **Get ready to open your haunted house!** Do you have snacks and drinks for people? Have you invited everyone you wanted to come? Are your actors in place?

5 **Let the haunting begin!** Your haunted house is now open for business, and it's time to get scaring.

Chapter 6

FACING YOUR GHOSTS

I'm the ghost with
the most, babe.

—Beetlejuice,
Beetlejuice (1988)

Remember when we talked about ghosts in ancient mythology and classic literature? The ghost media of today—movies, television shows, video games, musicals, and so on—is built upon the ghost stories and beliefs of the past. So what does that look like, exactly? Let's find out!

YOUR FRIENDLY NEIGHBORHOOD GHOST

We've read plenty about scary ghosts, but what about friendly ones?

Created by Seymour Reit and Joe Oriolo, Casper the Friendly Ghost appeared first in a cartoon in 1945. But Casper met a new generation of fans with his movie debut, *Casper* (1995). In his various film and TV incarnations, Casper is a good-natured and kind ghost.

Casper isn't the only ghost to have graced television screens.

Other TV shows with ghostly characters include *Scooby Doo* (1969– present), *Gravity Falls* (2012), *Courage the Cowardly Dog* (1996), *Are You Afraid of the Dark* (1990), and *Ghostwriter* (1992–1995)—and we can't forget teenage human-ghost Danny Phantom from the Nickelodeon cartoon *Danny Phantom* (2004–2007).

These days, while ghosts are still very much the stuff of terrifying tales, how they're depicted in TV shows and films can vary quite a bit. They might be spooky, or funny, or relatable, or just plain weird!

Pocket Friends

Ghosts haunt video games, too: Boos from Nintendo's *Luigi's Mansion*, the ghosts from *Pac-Man*, and the Hero's Spirit from the Legend of Zelda series. And in *Pokémon*, you can catch at least eighteen types of Pokémon, and one of these types is ghost Pokémon! Ghost Pokémon tend to live in abandoned places, dark caves, or cemeteries. Sound familiar? Even in video games, ghosts aren't too different from those in legends of the past.

GHOSTBUSTERS

We mentioned *Ghostbusters* in Chapter 2, but we're back for another round of ghostbusting! This 1984 movie, directed by Ivan Reitman and written by Dan Aykroyd and Harold Ramis, follows a group of parapsychology scientists—Egon Spengler, Ray Stantz, and Peter Venkman—who encounter their first ghost at the New York Public

Library. (By the way, if you haven't been there, the New York Public Library is worth a visit—it's amazing.) The three scientists form the Ghostbusters to take out the paranormal beings roaming the city.

Ghostbusters is a much-beloved film, and for good reason. It's packed with incredible moments, an all-star cast, and spooky visuals. The movie became the highest-grossing movie of its time and the theme song was a hit, topping the charts for weeks. It spawned an animated TV series, action figures, costumes, video games, and comic books. What I love about *Ghostbusters* is the friendship that ties the story together. Busting ghosts with your friends? I can't imagine a more beautiful thing.

According to Science

Slimy green monsters might be fictional, but you know what's real? Ghost fungus! Though this poisonous mushroom isn't technically a ghost, it does possess bioluminescent properties. It grows in Australia and hangs around dead or dying trees.

Rebooting Ghostbusters

If we're talking about the legacy of *Ghostbusters*, we've got to talk about the movies that followed the original. In 2014, a reboot was announced. It would star four talented actresses as the new Ghostbusters: Leslie Jones, Melissa McCarthy, Kate McKinnon, and Kristen Wiig. The internet went wild. Some people were excited by the all-woman main cast, while others weren't so happy. The movie trailers were met with an intense backlash online. Why? Sexism. The original 1984 film was special to many, but some people didn't want *Ghostbusters* to get an update for a new generation.

Ironically, women are at the center of many ghost stories, from ancient folk tales to modern-day urban legends. That includes movies about ghosts, like *The Haunting* (1963), *The Orphanage* (2007), and *Paranormal Activity* (2007), which all feature women dealing with the supernatural. A women-led *Ghostbusters* movie makes perfect sense! Unfortunately, the reaction to the announcement of the 2016 *Ghostbusters* movie wasn't the first or last time that a movie or TV show faced backlash for moving with the times.

The good news is that every year, there are more and more movies and TV shows that feature all kinds of people in all kinds of roles. On TV, you might find: a nonbinary pirate (played by Vico Ortiz on the TV series *Our Flag Means Death*), a Black mermaid (played by Halle Bailey in the 2023 live-action *Little Mermaid* movie), or a Muslim superheroine (played by Iman Vellani in the TV show *Ms. Marvel*). So if anyone ever tells you that you can't be whoever you want to be because of who you are—well, they're dead wrong.

IRL Ghost Hunting

In the early 2000s, ghost hunters went prime time with the advent of paranormal-investigation reality TV. In these shows, ghost hunters travel to different locations to investigate whether a place or object is truly haunted. MTV's *Fear*, *Most Haunted*, *Ghost Hunters*, *Paranormal State*, *Ghost Adventures*, and *Ghost Lab* led the charge. But it was the show *BuzzFeed Unsolved* that took the internet by storm.

Created and developed by Ryan Bergara, *BuzzFeed Unsolved* hit YouTube in 2016. Originally focusing on true crime, *BuzzFeed Unsolved* eventually expanded to include the supernatural, including—you guessed it—ghosts. In the show, Ryan and his cohost, Shane Madej, visited a location, explained to viewers the location's haunted history, and tried to document some paranormal activity.

A massive hit, the show wrapped up in 2021. But that wasn't the end. A new ghost-hunting series titled *Ghost Files* premiered in 2022.

Library Scavenger Hunt

Curious about literary ghosts? Try out this scavenger hunt at your local library to find your next favorite spine-chilling read. And be sure to ask the librarian if you have questions! They're there to help you out. (Librarians are some of my favorite people, if you can't tell.)

CAN YOU FIND THESE BOOKS?

1. A series about a ghost in a library

2. A book about a shy ghost

3. A graphic novel about a girl who has a ghost friend

4. A book about a ghost eating chips

5. A book written by Neil Gaiman (with ghosts!)

6. A graphic novel by Reimena Yee

7. A book with scary stories

8. A book about a girl facing the ghosts haunting her brother

9. A book series written by R. L. Stine

10. A nonfiction book that teaches you all about ghosts

ANSWER KEY:

1. The Haunted Library series by Dori Hillestad Butler

2. *Gustavo, the Shy Ghost* by Flavia Z. Drago

3. *Anya's Ghost* by Vera Brosgol

4. *The Adventures of the Bailey School Kids: Ghosts Don't Eat Potato Chips* by Debbie Dadey and Marcia Thornton Jones

5. *The Graveyard Book* by Neil Gaiman

6. *Séance Tea Party* by Reimena Yee

7. *Scary Stories to Tell in the Dark* by Alvin Schwartz

8. *Spirit Hunters* by Ellen Oh

9. The Goosebumps series by R. L. Stine

10. *Chilling with Ghosts: A Totally Factual Field Guide to the Supernatural* (the one you're holding right now!)

Read All About It

Looking for more ghostly fiction to read? Check out *The Girl and the Ghost* by Hanna Alkaf, *Just South of Home* by Karen Strong, *Ghost Squad* by Claribel Ortega, and *Too Bright to See* by Kyle Lukoff.

THE MORE YOU KNOW

Here's a little secret about paranormal investigation: you can do it, too! With a bit of research, you can learn all about the history of where you live and maybe uncover some haunted spots along the way.

To help you get started, consider these questions:

- When was my town founded?
- Who were the original residents of this land?
- What industries was this town historically known for?
- What notable figures used to live in my town?
- What historical spots or landmarks are in my town? What's the story behind them?
- Are there any ghost stories or urban legends about my town?

And if your research takes you to a cemetery or graveyard, be safe and respectful. That means following the cemetery rules, speaking quietly, and visiting with a friend or family member—don't go alone!

Conclusion

SO, DO YOU BELIEVE IN GHOSTS?

A ghost can be a lot
of things. A memory, a
daydream, a secret. Grief,
anger, guilt. But in my
experience, most times they're
just what we want to see.

—Steven Crain, *The Haunting
of Hill House* (2018)

You've reached the end of this guide! Can you believe it? I'm going to miss being on this supernatural adventure with you. But before we part ways, I have a final question for you: do you believe in ghosts?

SO, DO YOU?

You might be thinking, "Didn't you ask this question at the beginning?" And you're right! But now that we've reached the end of this book all about ghosts, I'm curious about what you think. This is your chance to take a moment and digest what you've read.

There's a lot to think about. You've learned what makes ghosts . . . well, ghosts! You've read up on ancient mythology and classic literature. You've uncovered the science and history behind why people may or may not believe in ghosts. And you've picked up your own tools for researching and better understanding the world around you.

So do you believe in ghosts? Actually, you know what, don't tell me. Whatever conclusion you come to, that's your decision. I'm just glad you're thinking about it. After all, it's important to understand what you believe and why. It isn't always easy, but it's crucial to understanding who you are.

Ghost stories come from a very real place. They come from a desire to give meaning to death and lend weight to the past. They might be scary (or funny!) tales, but they're also powerful reminders of our history, our cultural traditions, our personal beliefs, and what we hold dear. Ghost stories also help us face our fears. When we can share stories with other people about something that scares us, it makes that thing less scary. Life and death can be terrifying at times, but you know what? You're not alone. We're in this together.

OKAY, COOL. WHAT NOW?

I leave that up to you! If this guide has helped you think about the world in a new way, then I'm happy to hear it. And if you want to learn more about the world, supernatural or not, one good place to look is the past. In the past, you'll find not just history but also epic sagas, bizarre tales, and, yes, lots of ghost stories. The past is a ghoulishly great way to understand the present.

Read, research, and follow up on any and all questions you might have, no matter how weird or spooky they are. You never know what you might find!

BIBLIOGRAPHY

*Here lie the sources consulted in the
writing of this guide to all things ghostly.*

Bergara, Ryan. "The Mysterious Death of the Somerton Man Revisited." *Buzzfeed Unsolved: True Crime*, YouTube, April 17, 2020. Accessed November 6, 2022. https://www.youtube.com /watch?v=RLNTGsxvsao.

Claybourne, Anna. *Don't Read This Book Before Bed: Thrills, Chills, and Hauntingly True Stories*. Washington, DC: National Geographic, 2017.

Ellis, Melissa Martin. *The Everything Ghost Hunting Book: Tips, Tools, and Techniques for Exploring the Supernatural World*. Avon, MA: Adams Media, 2014.

"Few Americans Blame God or Say Faith Has Been Shaken Amid Pandemic, Other Tragedies." Pew Research Center, November 23, 2021. Accessed November 6, 2022. https://www.pewresearch.org /religion/2021/11/23/few-americans-blame-god-or-say-faith-has -been-shaken-amid-pandemic-other-tragedies.

Ghost Hunting. Special issue, 2022.

Ghosts: The Truth Behind the Legends & Lore. Special issue, 2022.

Graves, Zachary. *Ghosts: The Complete Guide to the Supernatural*. New York: Chartwell Books, 2011.

Guiley, Rosemary. *The Encyclopedia of Ghosts and Spirits*. New York: Facts on File, 2007.

Homer. *The Odyssey*. Translated by D. C. H. Rieu and E. V. Rieu. New York: Penguin Publishing Group, 2010.

Mark, Joshua J. "Ancient Egyptian Burial." *World History Encyclopedia*, January 19, 2013. Accessed November 6, 2022. https://www.worldhistory.org/Egyptian_Burial.

———. "Burial." *World History Encyclopedia*, September 2, 2009. Accessed November 6, 2022. https://www.worldhistory.org/burial.

———. "Religion in the Ancient World." *World History Encyclopedia*, March 23, 2018. Accessed November 6, 2022. https://www.worldhistory.org/religion.

Matsuo Bashō. *Narrow Road to the Interior: And Other Writings*. Translated by Sam Hamill. Boston: Shambhala Publications, 2000.

Morton, Lisa. *Calling the Spirits: A History of Seances*. London: Reaktion Books, 2021.

———. *Ghosts: A Haunted History*. London: Reaktion Books, 2017.

Newman, Kim. "The Main Types of Ghost Story, and How to Recognize Them." *Gizmodo*, October 9, 2014. Accessed November 6, 2022.

Ogden, Tom. *The Complete Idiot's Guide to Ghosts and Hauntings*. Indianapolis: Alpha Books, 1999.

Owens, Susan. *The Ghost: A Cultural History*. London: Harry N. Abrams, 2019.

Roland, Paul. *The Complete Book of Ghosts*. New York: Chartwell Books, 2007.

Walsh, Liza Gardner. *Ghost Hunter's Handbook*. Lanham, MD: Down East Books, 2016.

Winterbottom, Julie. *Frightlopedia: An Encyclopedia of Everything Scary, Creepy, and Spine-Chilling, from Arachnids to Zombies*. New York: Workman, 2016.

World's Scariest Places. Special issue, 2022.